DOODLE YOUR DAY

ANITA WOOD

Drawings by Jennifer Kalis

GIBBS SMITH
TO ENRICH AND INSPIRE HUMANKIND

For Madge who encouraged,
Suzanne who empowered,
and Michelle who always listens.
Thank You.
—Anita

For Paula, whose support helps me
feel less alone on my journey as an
ordinary parent of a special child.
And for Elliot, my doodle tester.
—Jennifer

Manufactured in Hong Kong, China,
in February 2013 by Toppan

First Edition

17 16 15 14 13   5 4 3 2

Published by Gibbs Smith
P.O. Box 667
Layton, Utah 84041

1.800.835.4993 orders
www.gibbs-smith.com

Designed by Jennifer Kalis
Manufacutured in Hong Kong, China, in February 2013 by Toppan printing.

Gibbs Smith books are printed on either recycled, 100% post-consumer waste, FSC-certified papers or on paper produced from sustainable PEFC-certified forest/controlled wood source. Learn more at www.pefc.org.

ISBN 13: 978-1-4236-2368-7

DOODLING your **way** through

EVERY **DAY** of the Year.

These DOODLES belong to:

NAME: _____

Address: _____

PHONE: _____

E-mail: _____

HAPPY NEW YEAR!

Doodle a bunch of confetti.

JANUARY 2

DOODLE A SNOWMAN ON THIS PAGE INSTEAD OF GOING OUT IN THE COLD.

THiS is what I HAD for LUNCH TODAY.

"Wacky Word" of the Day: "Bamboozle,"

which means to deceive.

See if you can use this in a sentence.

IT'S NATIONAL BIRD DAY!

Happy Bird Day to you! Doodle your favorite tweeter.

Cuddle Up Day!

Doodle some designs on this warm, fuzzy blanket.

My day iN 20 words or less:

JANUARY 8

Bubble Bath Day.

Fill the tub with bubbles and a rubber ducky.

JANUARY 9

TODAY I LEARNED SOMETHING NEW...

HOUSEPLANT APPRECIATION DAY

← Give this pot a happy plant.

STEP in a PuddLE and SPLaSh YouR FRiEnD Day.

Doodle a fun design on these galoshes.

Useless stuff that occupies my mind...

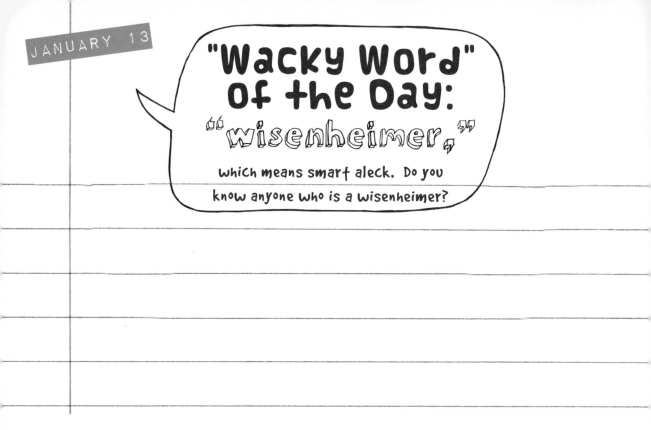

"Wacky Word"
of the Day:
"wisenheimer,"

which means smart aleck. Do you
know anyone who is a wisenheimer?

JANUARY 14

Dress Up Your Pet Day.

Give this pooch a fancy outfit.

National Hat Day.

Doodle an outrageous one here.

THIS is what I HAD for LUNCH TODAY.

What caught your eye today?

See the beauty all around you.

This Made Me Smile Today.

National Popcorn Day.

Buttered, caramel, or cheesy? Fill the bowl with your favorite kind.

Penguin Awareness Day.

Give this little fellow a fancy tuxedo.

National ♥ Hugging Day.

Who's your favorite person to hug?

"Wacky Word" of the Day:

"watchamacallit,"

which means an object whose name you can't remember. Use this word in a sentence.

MEASURE YOUR FEET DAY.

Come back to this entry next year to see how much they've grown!

STORMS

What's the Weather like today?

cloudy

windy

snowy

hot

Rain

Opposite Day.

Doodle something fun using your left hand. If you're a southpaw, use your right hand!

Stuff I did TODAY...

clip out a story from today's
newspaper that you found
interesting and stick it here!

Today, Lose Yourself in a Book.

Doodle the title of the one you're reading.

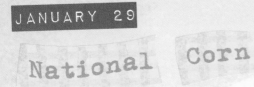

National Corn Chip Day.

What is your favorite way to eat them?

Find a quiet spot, look out the window, and doodle what you see.

Backward Day.

write a top-secret message ... backward.

"Wacky Word"
of the Day:
"dillydally,"
which means to waste time.

How do you like to dillydally?

Groundhog Day.

Did Punxsutawney Phil see his shadow today?

DRAW his shadow.

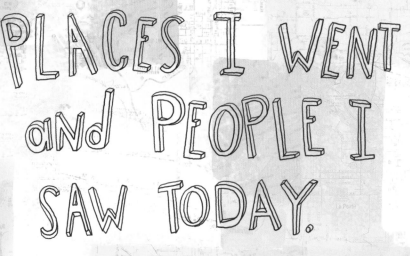

PLACES I WENT
and PEOPLE I
SAW TODAY.

PLACES I'D LIKE TO GO and PEOPLE I'D LIKE TO SEE.

National Weatherperson's Day, What was the weather like today?

CHECK OUT THE STORE ADS IN THE NEWSPAPER. CUT OUT A PICTURE OF SOMETHING YOU DESPERATELY WANT, AND STICK IT HERE!

THiS is what I HAD for LUNCH TODAY.

KITE FLYING DAY.

Doodle a design on this kite.

LISTEN UP!

is a WoRd I kept heaRing all day.

"Wacky Word" of the Day: "shenanigans,"

which means mischief. Is there somebody you know who is constantly up to shenanigans.

Are there any old keys laying around the house that aren't being used?

Paste one here and write a story about what you'd like this key to unlock.

Is there something you don't like?

How would you change it?

STUFF I PACK
FOR SCHOOL EVERY DAY!

Valentine's Day.

Who or what
do you love?

National Gumdrop Day.

Doodle a little family of gumdrops and their pets.

TODAY I LEARNED SOMETHING NEW...

It's the little things that count. Look around you and doodle some of the little things that you don't usually pay attention to.

"Wacky Word"
of the Day:
"flibbertigibbet,"
which is a silly word meaning a silly person.
Use this word in a sentence.

THiS is what I HAD for Lunch TODAY.

What makes you feel better when you're sick?

**IT'S MY DAY.
I CAN DOODLE WHAT I WANT TO.**

Stuff I wanted
to do TODAY...

International Dog Biscuit Appreciation Day.

what flavors do you think dog biscuits should come in? Doodle a few.

February is American Heart Month.
fill the space with hearts.

CARNIVAL DAY

Draw yourself as a
slideshow attraction at
a carnival. Would you be a
wolf boy, a bearded lady, the
world's tallest person, the world's
shortest person, or something else?

No-Brainer Day.

What kind of test would
be a "no-brainer" for you?

PUBLIC SLEEPING DAY.

Doodle a crazy place where you'd like to take a nap.

Why does today happen only once every four years?
See what you can find out, and then write about it.

National PEANUT BUTTER Lover's Day.

What's your favorite way to eat it—
straight out of the jar, with bananas, or with jam?

Old Stuff Day.
Find something old
(other than your dad!)
and stick it here.

If Pets Had Thumbs Day.

If they could send you a text message, what would it say?

"Wacky Word" of the Day: "squiggle,"

which means to squirm and wriggle.

Doodle something squiggling.

THiS iS what I HAD for Lunch TODAY.

National
FROZEN
Food Day.

Popsicles? Ice cream? Waffles?
Doodle your favorite.

Find a jigsaw puzzle
piece and stick it here.
Draw more pieces
around it.

TODAY I LEARNED SOMETHING NEW...

MARCH 9

PANIC DAY.

Doodle a panic button.
What throws you into a panic?

 Middle Name Pride Day.

Write your middle name.
If you don't have one, make one up.

Johnny Appleseed Day.

Give this worm a big juicy apple to eat.

Clip out your daily horoscope
from today's newspaper
and stick it here.

EARMUFF DAY.

Is it cold enough to wear earmuffs today?
Doodle some cool-looking earmuffs.

Brrr...

winter...

National Potato Chip Day.

You know you can't stop eating them! Draw your favorite kind.

ABSOLUTELY INCREDIBLE KID DAY.

Doodle yourself an amazing award,
because you are an absolutely incredible kid!

Everything You Do Is Right Day.

What did you do today?

SUBMARINE DAY.

Doodle either an underwater boat or your fav sandwich—
or some combination of the two!

"Wacky Word" of the Day: "hootenanny," which is a type of folk music concert. Doodle some instruments you'd expect to see at a hootenanny.

What's the weather like today?

STORMS

RAIN

SNOW

hot

Rain

cloudy

windy

My day in 10 words or less:

This Made Me Happy Today.

MARCH 22

INTERNATIONAL GOOF OFF DAY.

Doodle anything you want.

THiS is What I HAD for Lunch TODAY.

Draw an army of chocolate-covered raisins.

National Chocolate-Covered Raisin Day.

Waffle Day.

How do you like to eat them?

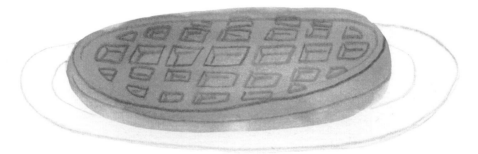

MARCH 26

MAKE UP YOUR OWN HOLIDAY DAY.

What would you like to celebrate?

I FOUND THIS ON
the WAY to SCHOOL.

Stick it here.

SOMETHING ON A STICK DAY.

Doodle all your favorite foods on a stick or toothpick.

Stuff I want to do TOMORROW...

"Wacky Word" of the Day: "aardvark,"

which is a large, burrowing, nocturnal animal. Doodle yourself an aardvark!

TODAY I LEARNED SOMETHING NEW...

APRIL 1

APRIL FOOL'S DAY!

Did you get "punked" today?

INTERNATIONAL CHILDREN'S BOOK DAY.

Doodle the cover
of your favorite book.

Rummage through your junk drawer
and stick something here that you've
forgotten about.

HEY, TODAY has 25 HOURS in it instead of 24. What will you do with the Extra hour?

GO For Broke Day.
Luck is on your side today.
What would you take a chance on?

Sorry Charlie Day.

It happens to all of us.
Have you ever been rejected?

What's the weather like today?

storms snowy hot cloudy windy

Draw a picture of a **Bird** Day.

Name Yourself Day.
Write your new name.

HELLO
my name is

National Sibling Day

Doodle a picture of you with your brothers and/or sisters.

THiS is what I HAD for LUNCH TODAY.

BIG WIND DAY.

Doodle the craziest thing you'd like to see blowing around in the sky.

What's the highest scoring word you can think of?

International Moment of Laughter Day.

what made you laugh today?

Rubber Eraser Day.

Doodle a bunch of fun-shaped erasers.

"Wacky Word"
of the Day:
"indubitably,"
which means without a doubt.

Try to use this in a sentence.

Put a DOLLAR $
Bill in an
Envelope and
Stick it here.

Try to keep adding to your
little stash of cash.

INTERNATIONAL JUGGLER'S DAY.

Doodle
yourself juggling
some water balloons.

NATIONAL GARLIC DAY.

SURE TO KEEP THE VAMPIRES AWAY!
DOODLE A VAMP FRIGHTENED
BY YOUR GARLIC NECKLACE.

LOOK Alike Day.
Let's combine this with the
"Wacky Word" of the Day:
"doppelganger,"
which means a person's double or
"look-alike." Doodle your doppelganger.
(Say that three times really fast!)

TODAY I LEARNED SOMETHING NEW...

National Jelly Bean Day.

Doodle some funny jelly bean people.

WORLD LABORATORY DAY.

Draw something oozing out of this beaker.

Pig in a Blanket Day.

A hot dog wrapped in dough, or a piggy snuggled up in a blanket?
Doodle whichever one you'd like to celebrate.

Stuff I did TODAY...

National
PRETZEL
Day

Twisted up, or straight and salty? Doodle your favorite kind.

BABE RUTH DAY.

Celebrate this legend of baseball
by eating a Baby Ruth candy bar
and sticking the wrapper here.

GREAT POETRY Reading Day.

Do you have a favorite poem? Why don't you write your own?

THiS is what I HAD for Lunch TODAY.

NATIONAL HONESTY DAY.

Have you ever told a lie? Why and to whom?

mother Goose Day.

Doodle your favorite nursery rhyme character.
(or make one up!)

TODAY LET'S PRETEND YOU
WOKE UP IN ANOTHER COUNTRY.
WHICH ONE?

If you owned a CANDY STORE, what would be your favorite thing to SELL?

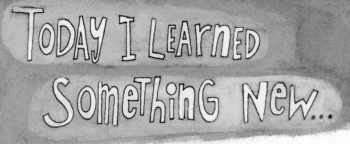

TODAY I LEARNED SOMETHING NEW...

BEVERage DAY.

What's your most favorite thing
to drink in the whole world?

"Wacky Word"
of the Day:
"horsefeathers,"
which means nonsense or rubbish.

Doodle a horse covered in feathers!

TODAY I am...

Lost Sock Memorial Day

Doodle a bunch of mismatched socks.

Clean Up Your Room Day.

Think of it as looking for buried treasure. What did you find?

EAT WHAT YOU WANT DAY.

If you could eat anything, what would you have for breakfast, lunch, dinner, and all the snacks you wanted?

THiS is what I HAD for LuNCH TODAY.

My day iN 5 words or less:

♪ DaNCe Like A ♪
♪ CHiCKeN Day. ♪

What does a chicken look like when it dances? Doodle one.

National Chocolate Chip Day.

Do you love 'em in cookies, cakes, or straight out of the bag?
Draw something with chocolate chips in it.

NATIONAL SEA MONKEY DAY.

Don't have one? Tell your mom and dad to get you a kit.
or doodle some in this little tank.

What's the longest word you know how to spell?

MAY 18

"Wacky Word" of the Day: "conniption,"

which means a tantrum, or something worse than a hissy fit. Do you know anybody who likes to have a conniption every now and then?

MAY 19

STORMS

What's the Weather like today?

cloudy

snowy

windy

hot

Rain

Be a Millionaire Day.

What is the first thing you would buy with all that money?

TODAY I LEARNED SOMETHING NEW...

BUY A MUSICAL INSTRUMENT DAY.

TONE

KEY

What instrument would you love to play?
Draw it.

music

Lucky Penny Day.

Keep your eyes peeled for one, and if you find one, stick it here.

WHAT'S YOUR FAVORITE KIND OF BUG?

Doodle it here.

National Brown-Bag-It Day.
What did you pack for lunch?

MAY 26

THiS is what I HAD for DinneR TODAY.

My B.F.F.

Stick a picture of
him or her on this page
and doodle around it.

Fun STUff I want to do this SummeR:

"Wacky Word"
of the Day:
"discombobulated,"
which means confused or out of sorts.

Use this in a sentence.

Water a Flower Day.
Doodle a bunch of flowers.

MAY 31

STORMS

What's the Weather like today?

cloudy

snow

windy

hot

Rain

JUNE 1

Heads I win, tails you lose! Doodle your own designs on this Coin.

Flip a Coin Day

Stick a piece of your favorite gum here in case of emergency.

find a pattern or design that you like and repeat it here.

HUG YOUR CAT DAY.

DRAW YOUR CUDDLY CAT.
IF YOU DON'T HAVE ONE, DOODLE YOUR OWN.

National Gingerbread Day.

Doodle a gingerbread house and decorate it with your favorite candies.
(I know - it's summertime, not Christmas!)

TODAY I LEARNED SOMETHING NEW...

National Chocolate Ice Cream Day

Is there anything better?!
(If there is, draw it.)

"Wacky Word" of the Day:

"hoi polloi,"

which means the common people, or the general population. Use this in a sentence.

A doodle a day keeps the boredom away.

THIS is What I HAD for LUNCH TODAY.

This Made Me Smile Today.

It's your day and you can do anything you want! What would you do?

STORMS

SNOWY

hot

What's the weather like today?

cloud

wind

FavoRite **THINGS** I like about SUMMERTIME.

Smile Power Day.

Doodle some different smiley faces.

You are here.

*

Draw a map of your hometown that shows where you live.

EAT YOUR VEGETABLES DAY.

Doodle your favorite veggies.

Go Fishing Day!

If you can't go, then doodle some
fish trying to avoid your hook!

"Wacky Word" of the Day:

"quagmire,"

which means a sticky situation or
predicament. Use this in a sentence.

Ice Cream Soda Day.

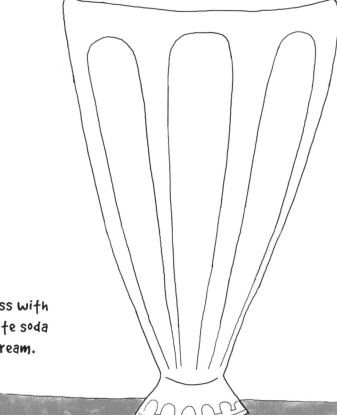

Fill the glass with
your favorite soda
and ice cream.

School might be out, but that doesn't mean you can't learn something new.
Do a little investigative work and find out what happened on this day in history.

THIS is What I HAD for LUNCH TODAY.

NATIONAL PINK DAY.

Wear it, chew it, doodle with it.

I wish...

National Log Cabin Day.

Draw one here. What famous president grew up in a log cabin?

National Chocolate Pudding Day.

Doodle yourself with a chocolate mustache.

SUNGLASSES DAY.

Doodle a hot pair of shades.

PAUL BUNYAN DAY.

Who is Paul Bunyan, you ask?
Well, do some digging and see what you can learn.

STORMS

What's the Weather like today?

cloudy

windy

snowy

hot

Rain

"Wacky Word" of the Day:

"snollygoster,"

which means a crooked person or swindler.

Doodle a crooked person.

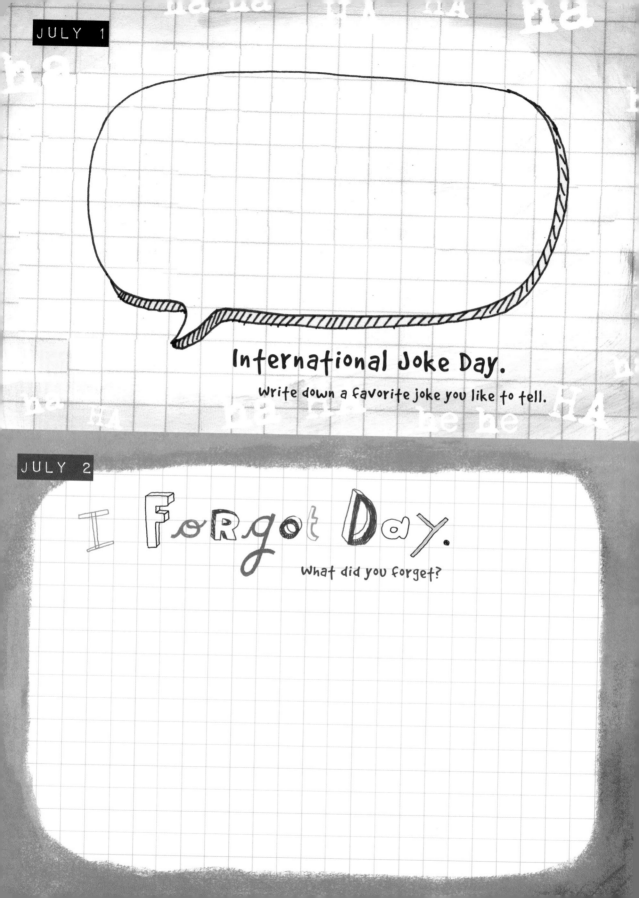

International Joke Day.

Write down a favorite joke you like to tell.

I Forgot Day.

What did you forget?

THiS is what I HAD for Lunch TODAY.

Sidewalk Egg Frying Day.

Was it really that hot today? Doodle an egg frying on the sidewalk!

TODAY I LEARNED SOMETHING NEW...

National Fried Chicken Day.

Doodle a chick that's gotten way too much sun!

National Macaroni Day

Doodle a picture using macaroni shapes.

Map it out. Where did you go today?

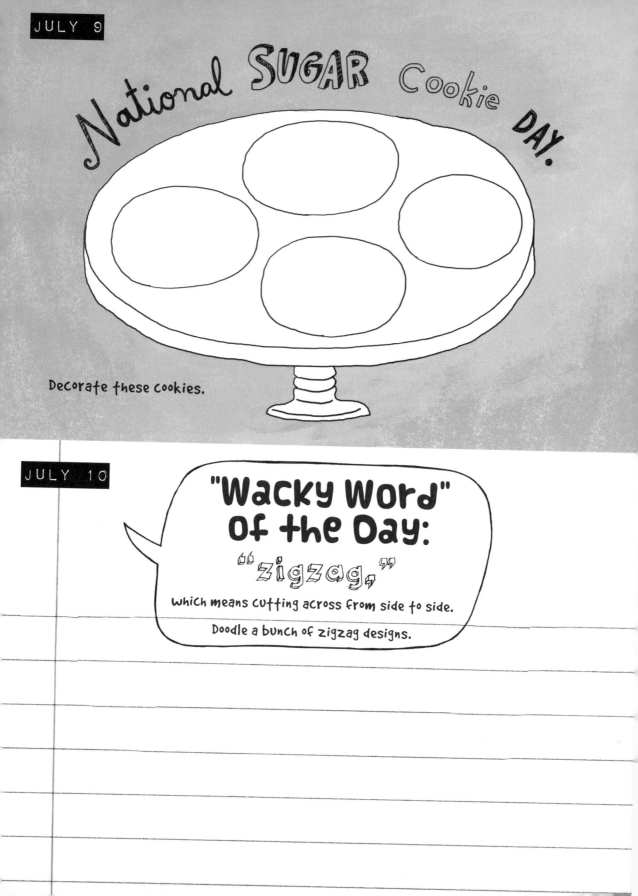

JULY 9

National SUGAR Cookie DAY.

Decorate these cookies.

JULY 10

"Wacky Word"
of the Day:
"zigzag,"
which means cutting across from side to side.

Doodle a bunch of zigzag designs.

CUT OUT WORDS FROM A MAGAZINE
AND WRITE A MESAGE TO YOUR FUTURE SELF.
STICK 'EM HERE.

DiffeRent CoLoRed Eyes Day.

What crazy color would you choose?

We all have oUR  GeeKY NeRdY SiDes.

What makes you a geek?

cow appreciation Day.

What do you love about cows?

THiS is what I HAD for Lunch TODAY.

JULY 17

National Peach Ice Cream Day

With or without the fuzz?

TODAY I LEARNED SOMETHING NEW...

Start a collection of movie ticket stubs and stick 'em here.

National Lollipop Day.

How many licks until you reach the stick?

NATIONAL JUNK Food Day.

Doodle your favorites.

I want...

NATIONAL HOT DOG DAY.

Mustard or ketchup?

Stick Something **RED** Here.

Hot Fudge Sundae Day.

With cherries, nuts, and whipped cream please!

Aunt and Uncle Day.

Do you have a favorite you'd like to tell about?

TAKE YOUR PANTS FOR A WALK DAY. ?

Where did you go?

National Hamburger Day.

I like mine with...

National Lasagna Day

Doodle a secret message on this lasagna noodle.

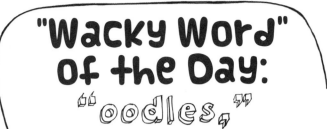

"Wacky Word" of the Day: "oodles,"

which means lots and lots.

Doodle oodles of big and little dots.

TODAY I LEARNED SOMETHING NEW...

THIS is What I HAD for Lunch TODAY.

National ICE CREAM SANDWICH Day.

Make sure you eat at least one to celebrate!
What's your fav?

National Watermelon ay.

Enjoy a slice of watermelon today, stick some of the
seeds here, or plant a couple and see if they grow.

AUGUST 4

What's the Weather like today?

STORMS
SNOWY
hot
Rain
cloudy
windy

AUGUST 5

THIS MADE ME HAPPY:

Wiggle Your Toes Day.

Draw happy little faces on these toes.

Stick Something BlUE Here.

WHAT KIND OF ANIMAL are YOU?

BOOK LOVER'S DAY.

What's your favorite one that your mom used to read to you before bedtime? How many times have you read it?

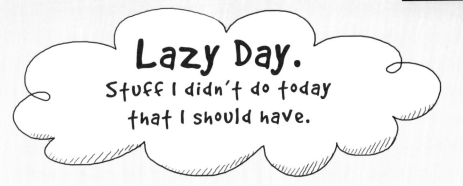

Lazy Day.
Stuff I didn't do today that I should have.

THIS is what I HAD for Lunch TODAY.

Give your favorite celebrity a makeover by sticking a picture of the person here and give him or her some buck teeth, a beard; you get the idea!

AUGUST 13

Left Hander's Day.
All right hander's, doodle with your left hand.

National Lemon Meringue Pie Day

Doodle your best lemon pucker face.

National Tell a Joke Day.

Another chance to write down one of your favorite jokes.

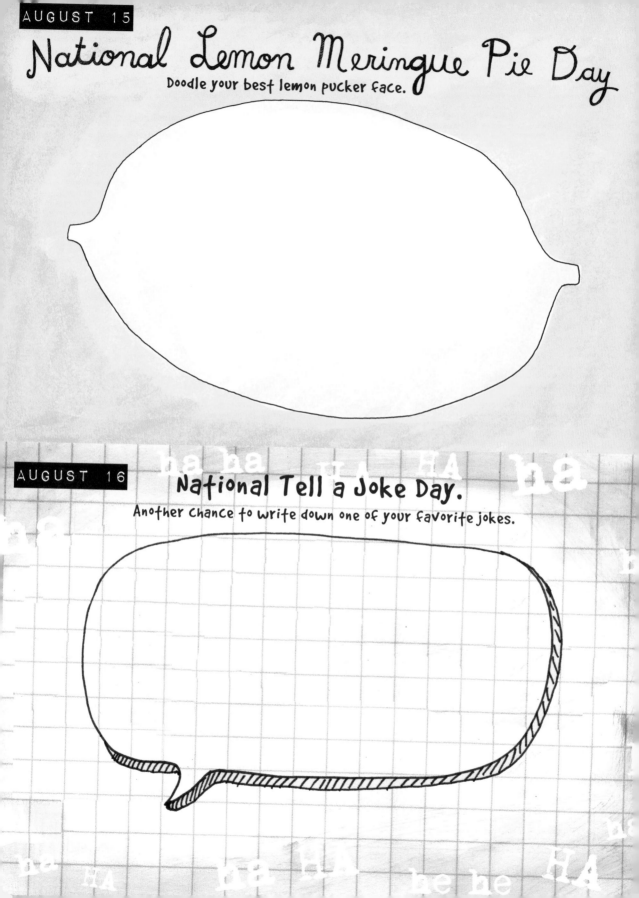

"Wacky Word"
of the Day:
"highfalutin,"

which means fancy.

Try to use this word in a sentence.

WHAT KIND OF CEREAL ARE YOU?

AUGUST is NATIONAL PICNIC MONTH.

Doodle some of the ants that came to join you on your picnic.

TODAY I LEARNED SOMETHING NEW...

Be an Angel Day.

Stick a picture of yourself here and doodle some wings and a halo around it.

Ride the Wind Day.

Where would you like it to take you?

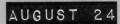

THiS iS what I HAD for LUNCH TODAY.

The password for today is...

NATIONAL CHERRY POPSICLE DAY.

Doodle some big cherry red lips.

fun things I did this summer.

Are you excited to get back to school?
What is your favorite class or subject?

"Wacky Word"
Of the Day:
"buffoon,"

which means clown.

Doodle a silly looking clown.

National Toasted marshmallow Day.

A good time to soften up one of your peeps
left over from Easter! Doodle a few.

National Trail Mix Day.

What are your favorite ingredients besides M&M's?

TODAY I LEARNED SOMETHING NEW...

This is what I Had for Breakfast.

September is Better Breakfast Month.

SEPTEMBER is also Hispanic Heritage Day.

Learn how to say something in Spanish.

Newspaper Carrier Day.
Stick your favorite
newspaper cartoon here.

If only...

Fight Procrastination day.

What is something you always put off doing until the last minute?

NEITHER RAIN NOR SNOW DAY.

Leave a note in your mailbox for your mail carrier thanking him/her for doing such a good job. Doodle a fun stamp design on it.

"Wacky Word" of the Day:

"serendipity,"

which means good fortune or luck. Doodle some good luck symbols like a ladybug or a four-leaf clover. What other symbols can you learn about?

TEDDY BEAR DAY.

Do you have a favorite teddy? Draw his/her picture.

Swap Ideas Day.

Do some brainstorming with your friends and write down all your cool ideas.

No News Is Good News Day.

Stick today's newspaper headline here.

THiS is What I HAD for LUNCH TODAY.

DEFY SUPERSTiTiON DAY.

Black cats, walking under a ladder, spilled salt, or the number 13?
What are you superstitious about?

Leaf it here.

Start a collection of leaves from the same tree and
stick a new one here as the colors start to change.

make a HAT DAY.

Grab some old newspaper and get to work folding one up.

TODAY I LEARNED SOMETHING NEW...

Constitution Day.

Write down the preamble.
I'll help you to get started...

We the People
of the United States,

"Wacky Word" of the Day:
"whippersnapper,"
which means someone who is unimportant.

Try to use this in a sentence.

International Talk Like a Pirate Day.

Doodle yourself wearing an eye patch.

What if...

World Gratitude Day.

Five things I am grateful for...

Elephant Appreciation Day.
What do you love about elephants?
Doodle one.

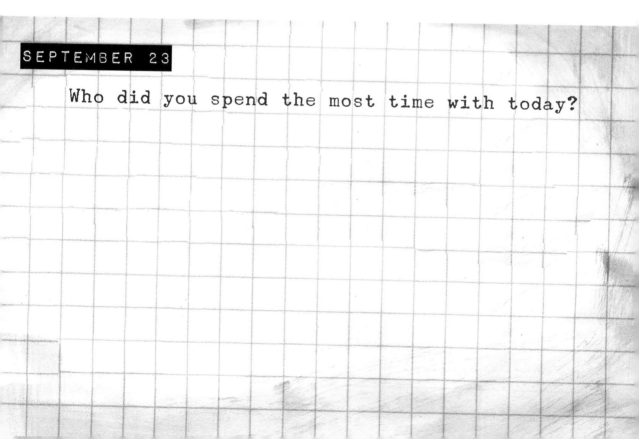

SEPTEMBER 23

Who did you spend the most time with today?

THiS is what I HAD for LUNCH TODAY.

NATIONAL COMIC BOOK DAY.

Do you have a favorite superhero?

National Pancake Day.

How many pancakes have you eaten at one time?

Storms

What's the weather like today?

cloudy

snowy

windy

hot

Rain

Ask a Stupid Question Day.

Need I say more?

"Wacky Word" of the Day: "skeedaddle,"

which means to run away fast.

Try to use this in a sentence.

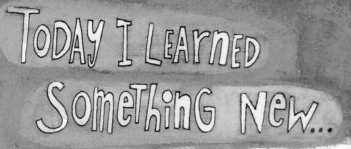

TODAY I LEARNED SOMETHING NEW...

OCTOBER 1

STick SOMETHING FUZZY Here.

(No, not your neighbor's cat!)

Name your Car Day.

You can do this now so you'll be prepared when you finally get one.

Doodle your dream car.

WHat ARE YOU
GOING TO BE FOR Halloween?

Start planning your costume now. Doodle it.

National Taco Day.

What are your favorite fillings?

DO SOMETHING NICE DAY.

What will you do and for whom?

MAD HATTER DAY.

LIKE THE CRAZY GUY IN ALICE IN WONDERLAND, DOODLE YOURSELF A BIG OLD TOP HAT.

BALD AND FREE DAY.

What would you look like without any hair?

"Wacky Word"
of the Day:
"periwinkle,"
which is a color in the blue-violet family.
Do you have a crayon this color?
Doodle something with it.

Curious Events Day.

Did anything strange happen today?

National Angel Food Cake Day.

Give this cake some wings and a halo.

IT'S MY PARTY DAY!

WHAT TYPE OF PARTY WOULD YOU THROW?

THiS is what I HAD for Lunch TODAY.

International Skeptics Day.

Is there something that you have a hard time believing?

Dictionary Day.

Pick up a dictionary, close your eyes, open to a random page and point with your finger. Write down the word you chose and its meaning.

wear something gaudy Day.

Gaudy means flashy, loud, or extravagant.
Doodle something that would make you stand out in a crowd.

N. BEARD DAY.

okay then, doodle yourself with a mustache!

"Wacky Word" of the Day: "kerfuffle,"

which means a big fuss.

Try to use this in a sentence.

I can...

Babbling Day.

Write a sentence that goes on and on about nothing in particular.

NATIONAL NUT DAY.

Doodle some of the nutty people in your life.

THiS is What
I HAD
for LunCH
TODAY.

TiME to START CARViNG SOME PUMPKiNS.
Doodle a few here while you're at it!

World Pasta Day.

We all love spaghetti, but what are some of your other favorite types of pasta? Doodle some fun shapes.

TODAY I LEARNED SOMETHING NEW...

Today I'm feeling like...

Come to your senses already. Doodle something you saw, heard, touched, smelled, and tasted today.

NATIONAL FRANKENSTEIN DAY:

Doodle a picture of the crazy monster here.

NaTiONaL Candy Corn Day.

Have your mom slice one in half (so your page won't be so lumpy) and stick it here. Doodle a bunch more.

LOOK FOR CIRCLES DAY.

They're everywhere. You can doodle a few too, if you like!

Sandwich Day.

Bite into your favorite one!

KING TUT DAY.

King Tutankhamun's tomb was discovered in Egypt on this day in 1922, full of amazing treasures. Doodle a few.

LET'S HAVE A CRAZY HAIR DAY.

How would you wear yours?

Marooned
Without a
Compass Day.

Doodle a
compass to
help you
find your
direction.

"Wacky Word"
of the Day:
"monkeyshines,"
which means a playful trick or prank.

Try to use this in a sentence.

See what you can learn about
"dunce caps" and then doodle one.

DUNCE DAY.

THiS is what
I HAD
for LUNCH
TODAY.

FORGET-ME-NOT Day.

Is there somebody special
you'd always like to remember?
Stick a picture of them here.

TODAY I LEARNED SOMETHING NEW...

Do you have questions about certain things that you'd like answers to, such as, Why is the sky blue? See what you can find out.

Predict your future twenty years from now.

Where do you live?

What kind of work do you do?

Are you married?

Where have you traveled?

Where were you and what were you doing today
at 4:15 this afternoon?

Clean YOUR Refrigerator Day.

Doodle some fruit or veggies that have grown a nice green coat of fur. Ewww!

Button Day.

Look around for some loose buttons
and stick them here.
Make some fun doodles with them.

WORLD PEACE Day.

How can you help promote peace in your home?

"Wacky Word"
of the Day:
"moxie,"

which means having courage or determination.

Do you know someone with a lot of moxie?

storms

cloudy

What's the
weather
like today?

snowy

windy

hot

Rain

Beautiful * Day.

What is beautiful to you?

WORLD HELLO DAY.

CAN YOU MAKE A FUN DOODLE
WITH THE WORD "HELLO"?

Make sure you greet everyone
you see with a nice hello.

GO FOR A RIDE DAY.

other than a car or a bus, doodle something else you would like to take a ride on.

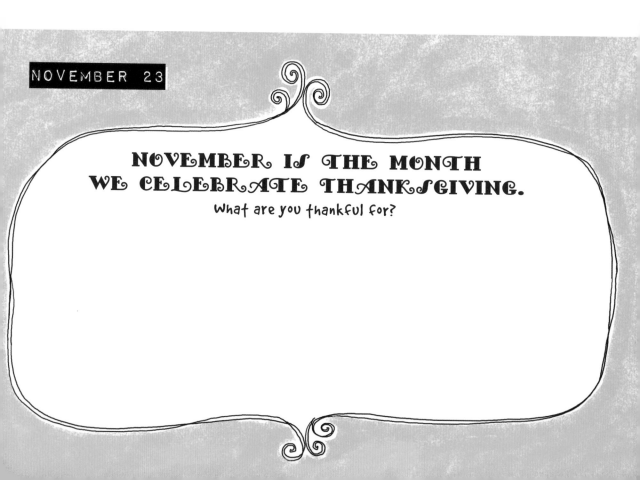

NOVEMBER IS THE MONTH
WE CELEBRATE THANKSGIVING.

What are you thankful for?

TODAY I LEARNED SOMETHING NEW...

THIS is what I HAD for Lunch TODAY.

National Cake Day.

cakes aren't just
for birthdays!

Give this one some
frosting and decorations.

Pins and Needles Day.

A day where everyone anxiously awaits something that hasn't
yet happened. Do you think you've made Santa's "Nice List"?

MAKE YOUR OWN HEAD DAY.

Doodle a picture of your head!

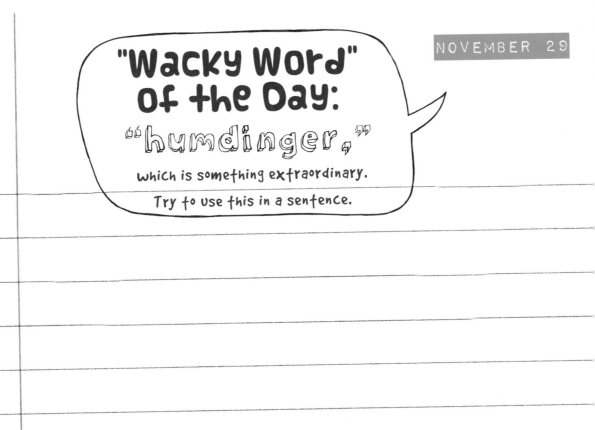

"Wacky Word" of the Day:

"humdinger,"

which is something extraordinary.

Try to use this in a sentence.

NatioNal mouSSe Day.

The dessert, not the animal!
Mousse is the French word for "foam."

DECEMBER 1

Eat a Red Apple Day, and while you're at it,
write a letter to a friend.

National Fritter's Day.

Fried cake or dough with fruit in it. Yum.

storms

clouds

What's the weather like today?

snowy

hot

windy

rain

SANTA'S LIST DAY.
Who would you put on the "Naughty List"?

What Kind of Christmas ornament are you?

St. Nicholas Day.

Doodle a picture of the jolly old fellow.

Five things your friends don't know about you.

THIS is What I HAD for Lunch TODAY.

DECEMBER 9

CHRISTMAS Card Day.

Design a card that you'd like to send to your friends.

"Wacky Word" of the Day: "chihuahua," which is a very small dog.

Doodle one.

TODAY I LEARNED SOMETHING NEW...

P✸insettia Day

This flower is recognized as a symbol of Christmas.
Doodle one.

DECEMBER 13

What kind of **Bird** are you?

All good things to those who wait.
What are you waiting for?

THINGS I WOULD WISH FOR MY FRIENDS AND FAMILY.

National Chocolate-Covered Anything  Day.

would you ever eat a chocolate-covered grasshopper?

THIS is what I HAD for LUNCH TODAY.

Bake Cookies Day.

what are your favorite kinds?

Look for an Evergreen Day.

Time to decorate the tree!

GO CAROLING DAY.

write down your favorite christmas carol.

DECEMBER 21

Today is the winter solstice, the shortest day of the year, so let's celebrate short things like stories, short school days, and short people. what other short things can you add to the list?

"Wacky Word" of the Day: *"fezziwig,"*

a character from Charles Dickens' *A Christmas Carol.* He's a happy sort of fellow who wears a large wig. Give him a crazy hairpiece.

STORMS

What's the Weather like today?

cloudy

snowy

windy

hot

Have a family member draw a
picture for you and stick it here.

Christmas Day.

Stick a piece of wrapping paper and ribbon here.
What surprise did it cover?

TODAY I LEARNED SOMETHING NEW...

Make Cut Out Snowflakes Day.

Stick a few of 'em here.

CARD PLAYING DAY.

Is there a card in the deck that doesn't have a mate? Stick it here!

PEPPER POT DAY.

Pepper Pot Soup was first made on Dec 29, 1777. Do a little research and find out more about this interesting soup.

HOW are YOU going to CELEBRATE on NEW YEAR'S EVE?

What will your NEW YEAR'S RESOLUTIONS BE?

Time for a new copy of this book!

My YEAR in REViEW:

Go back through the pages of this book and write down:

of all the different things you learned this year,

what was the most interesting?

Was there a pattern in the weather? Nice days versus icky ones?

Did you eat the same boring thing for lunch?

What was your favorite "Wacky Word"?